KAKAPOS

ON THE TRAIL

STUDYING
SECRETIVE
ANIMALS
IN THE WILD

by Joyce Markovics

CHERRY LAKE PRESS

Published in the United States of America by Cherry Lake Publishing Group
Ann Arbor, Michigan
www.cherrylakepublishing.com

Reading Adviser: Marla Conn, MS Ed., Literacy specialist, Read-Ability, Inc.
Content Adviser: Andrew Digby, PhD
Book Designer: Ed Morgan

Photo Credits: © Andrew Digby, cover and title page; © freepik.com, TOC; © Andrew Digby, 4–5; © Andrew Digby, 4; © Deidre Vercoe/New Zealand Department of Conservation, 5; © Andrew Digby, 6; © Andrew Digby, 7; Wikimedia Commons, 8; © Andrew Digby, 9; © Andrew Digby, 10; © Nature Picture Library/Alamy Stock Photo, 11 top; © Andrew Digby, 11 bottom; Wikimedia Commons, 12 left; Wikimedia Commons, 12 right; Wikimedia Commons, 13; © rook76/Shutterstock, 14; © Alan Tunnicliffe/Shutterstock, 15 top; © Naoki Nishio/Shutterstock, 15 bottom; Wikimedia Commons, 16; © Andrew Digby, 17; © Andrew Digby, 18; © Frans Lanting/Lanting.com, 19; © Andrew Digby, 20 top; Wikimedia Commons, 20 bottom; © Andrew Digby, 21; © Andrew Digby, 22; © Andrew Digby, 23; © Lydia Uddstrom, 24; © Andrew Digby, 25; © Andrew Digby, 26–27; © Metelitsa Viktoriya/Shutterstock, 28; © spatuletail/Shutterstock, 29; © Morphart Creation/Shutterstock, 31.

Cherry Lake Press is an imprint of Cherry Lake Publishing Group.

Library of Congress Cataloging-in-Publication Data
Names: Markovics, Joyce L., author.
Title: Kakapos / by Joyce L. Markovics.
Description: First edition. | Ann Arbor, Michigan : Cherry Lake Publishing, [2021] | Series: On the trail: studying secretive animals in the wild | Includes bibliographical references and index. | Audience: Ages 10 | Audience: Grades 4-6
Identifiers: LCCN 2020030349 (print) | LCCN 2020030350 (ebook) | ISBN 9781534180475 (hardcover) | ISBN 9781534182189 (paperback) | ISBN 9781534183193 (ebook) | ISBN 9781534181489 (pdf)
Subjects: LCSH: Kakapo—Juvenile literature.
Classification: LCC QL696.P7 M33 2021 (print) | LCC QL696.P7 (ebook) | DDC 598.7/1—dc23
LC record available at https://lccn.loc.gov/2020030349
LC ebook record available at https://lccn.loc.gov/2020030350

Printed in the United States of America
Corporate Graphics

CONTENTS

PECULIAR PARROTS

A gentle breeze was blowing as **conservation biologist** Andrew Digby headed up a forested hillside. He was on Whenua Hou, also known as Codfish Island, in New Zealand. Various plants and moss created a green carpet on the forest floor. Andrew scanned the area for a bird that's so rare and strange, few people know about it. It was a lucky day. Andrew found the bird he was looking for—an adult kakapo (kah-kah-POH).

A kakapo

"Kakapos are probably the weirdest birds in the world. They're large, **flightless**, **nocturnal** parrots," says Andrew. But before he spotted the bird, he smelled it. The scent was "strong but not unpleasant," he says. It's "sweet, earthy, and **musty**." Suddenly, he heard something.

Conservation biologist Andrew Digby with a kakapo

LOOK CLOSER

Kakapos are the only kind of parrots that cannot fly. They're found on just four small islands off the coast of New Zealand.

MEET A KAKAPO

On the ground, Andrew saw a plump, yellowish-green bird slowly walking. "Kakapos do everything slowly, including walking," Andrew says. The kakapo's **mottled** feathers blended in perfectly with its **habitat**. "Their **camouflage** is incredible."

The first time Andrew saw a kakapo, the bird's size surprised him. "They're big," he says, "much bigger than I expected." In fact, kakapos are the largest parrots in the world, weighing up to 9 pounds (4 kilograms)— as much as a gallon of milk!

A kakapo blends in with its forest home.

With the help of his teammate, Andrew carefully grabbed the slow-moving kakapo. The bird's name was Moss, and Andrew had captured the young male before. "We try and **minimize** handling as much as possible," says Andrew. However, once a year, he and his team safely catch all the birds on the island to check their health and make sure their **transmitters** are working.

Andrew holds a kakapo and checks its transmitter.

LOOK **CLOSER**

Each kakapo is fitted with a transmitter that looks like a tiny backpack. This device allows Andrew and his team to track the birds and monitor their activity.

FACE–TO–FACE

Andrew checked the transmitter, which was working fine. As he examined Moss, he peered into the bird's round eyes. The kakapo looked right back at him with curiosity. Kakapos have large, forward-facing eyes like owls. Their eyes help them see at night, which is when kakapos are most active. Another special feature is a round disk of feathers around each eye. The feathery disks help direct sound waves toward the birds' ears.

A kakapo's "whisker" feathers, or vibrissae

LOOK **CLOSER**

Kakapos have gray beaks. Whisker-like feathers called vibrissae (vye-BRIH-see) surround the beaks. These feathers help the birds feel around in the dark.

Moss was calm as Andrew gently touched his body. "Each kakapo has its own personality," says Andrew. "They range from friendly to grumpy or just plain **aloof**." Wild kakapos like Moss have been known to walk up to and climb on people. "There are some kakapos which aren't scared of people," he says.

A group of friendly kakapo chicks greets Andrew

FLIGHTLESS WONDER

Kakapos can't fly, but "they're excellent hikers with large, strong legs," Andrew says. Even though they do most everything slowly, they can run pretty fast. They move with leaping **strides**, almost like a jogger. When they run, they spread their wings. According to Andrew, "their wings are used for balance and more graceful falls."

Kakapos often use their wings for balance.

Kakapos are also good climbers and have strong claws on each foot. Their favorite food is found in rimu trees, which can be over 65 feet (20 meters) tall. To reach the rimu fruit, the parrots use their claws to climb up tree trunks and branches. Along the way, kakapos rely on their beaks almost like an extra claw to steady and pull themselves up. If they fall, they spread their wings, using them as a kind of **parachute**.

A kakapo climbing a tree

The fruit of the rimu tree

LOOK **CLOSER**

Kakapos are herbivores. They eat leaves, flowers, seeds, bark, fruit, and tubers.

A LONG HISTORY

Kakapos have been on Earth for about 30 million years. Scientists think that long ago, kakapos weighed less and could fly. However, they had few **predators**, and over time they **evolved**. As a result, "they gained weight and lost their flying ability," says Andrew.

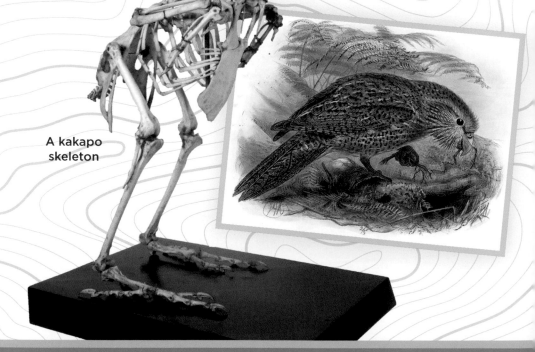

A kakapo skeleton

Before the arrival of humans, large numbers of parrots lived across New Zealand. Around 800 years ago, the Māori people settled in the area. They hunted kakapos for food and used their feathers to make cloaks. The Māoris also accidentally introduced rats to the islands. Kakapo eggs and chicks became food for the rats. Then, in the 1840s, European settlers arrived and nearly wiped out the kakapos.

Māori people dressed in feather cloaks

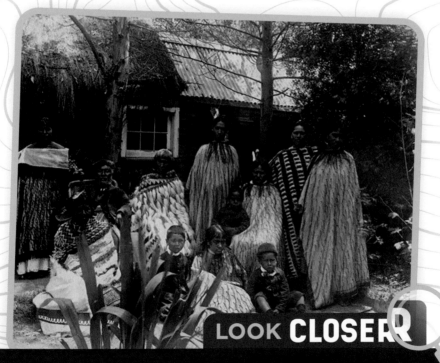

LOOK **CLOSER**

The word *kakapo* comes from the Māori terms *kākā* for "parrot" and *pō* for "night." It's often spelled kākāpō. The special accents are called macrons. They indicate a long vowel sound and honor the Māori culture!

NEAR EXTINCTION

The Europeans chopped down forests to make way for farms. This greatly reduced the overall amount of kakapo habitat. They also hunted the parrots for food. Even more damaging, the Europeans brought cats, dogs, and stoats with them. The flightless birds were easy prey for these animals. Within a few decades, the once plentiful kakapos were on the edge of **extinction**.

A stamp showing European settlers arriving in New Zealand in 1840

Stoats are a kind of weasel that can easily kill a flightless bird.

In 1974, no one knew if any kakapos were left, even after decades of searching. Eventually, two small groups of less than 200 birds were found. Scientists moved these remaining birds to islands to save them. The islands were free from cats, stoats, and other predators. They closely watched and studied the birds to make sure they did not go extinct.

When kakapos are in danger, they stand absolutely still. This made it even easier for predators to catch them.

MEETING UP

Other factors threaten kakapo survival. Kakapos are thought to live anywhere from 20 to 90 years. This would make them one of the longest-living birds in the world. However, the parrots don't start having young until they're 5 years old. Also, kakapos only **breed** when rimu trees are fruiting. This happens every 2 to 4 years.

An adult kakapo feeding

This is a male kakapo.

Another big challenge for kakapos is finding a **mate**. There are so few left that the birds have trouble finding a partner. And kakapos usually live alone. When the time comes to breed, however, males put on a big, loud show. This display can help them find the right female.

LOOK **CLOSER**

Male kakapos are larger than females. Females have a narrower head and beak.

MALE
CALLS

First, a male kakapo finds a big rock or hilltop. This usually happens in December. Then he makes a series of round **depressions** in the ground using his beak and claws. The male might create as many as 10 of these bowl-shaped hollows. All are connected by little trails, which he also makes.

This male kakapo is sitting in a hollow he made.

The male sits in one of the bowls. Then he sucks air into a special sac in his throat and makes a low booming call every couple of seconds. Often, the call can be heard for miles around. "It's a sound you almost feel rather than hear, since it's so low **frequency**," says Andrew. After the male booms 20 to 30 times, he makes a different sound called a ching. This sound helps lead females right to his location. The male repeats his booming and chinging all night, every night, for up to 3 months!

A male kakapo calls for a mate.

LOOK **CLOSER**

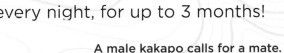

Scientists aren't sure why male kakapos create the hollows. They may provide shelter for the birds or help them make their calls louder.

FLUFFYCHICKS

Once the male attracts a female, they mate. She creates a nest in a hollow tree or in a small, rocky cave. There she lays between one and five eggs. After about 30 days, the eggs hatch. The babies are covered with fluffy, white down. The female raises the chicks entirely on her own.

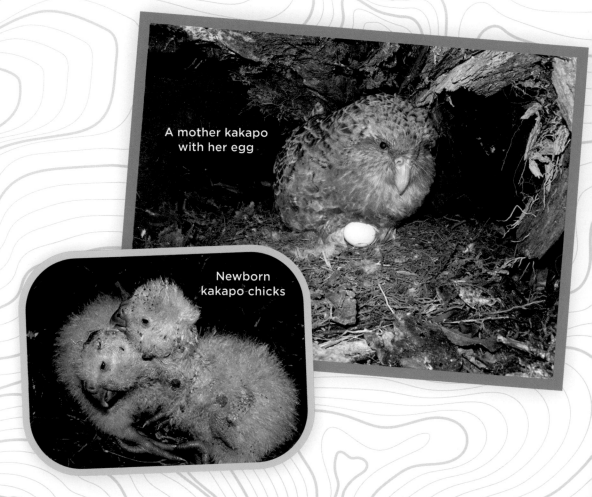

A mother kakapo with her egg

Newborn kakapo chicks

At night, the kakapo mother leaves her chicks to find food. The chicks eat lots of rimu fruit—over 1 pound (0.5 kg) each per night! The female has to work constantly to collect enough of the tiny fruits for her growing chicks. During this time, the babies are alone and defenseless. After about 10 weeks, the chicks have their adult feathers and are ready to leave the nest. However, they may stay near their mother for up to 6 months.

Older kakapo chicks

LOOK CLOSER

Sometimes, the mother can't feed all of her chicks or the chicks become sick. In that case, scientists step in. They take them from the nest and raise them in captivity. When the chicks are almost fully grown, they are released.

KAKAPO
RECOVERY

In 1989, scientists wrote the first Kakapo Recovery Plan. It described the bird **population** and what was being done for them. Then in 1995, when there were just 51 kakapos left, scientists formed the Kakapo Recovery Programme. The main goal of the group is to protect the **endangered** bird. Andrew and a team of other scientists and workers do this by caring for living kakapos, as well as increasing the population of the birds.

A kakapo named Sinbad

Because there are so few birds left, **inbreeding** is a major problem, according to Andrew. Birds that are too closely related often lay eggs that don't hatch. So Andrew and others remove a tiny amount of blood from each bird. The blood is analyzed for its **genetic** makeup. This helps the scientists learn more about the birds and match up individuals that will likely have healthy chicks.

Andrew examines a bird in the field.

LOOK CLOSER

About half of all kakapo eggs don't hatch, mostly due to inbreeding. The hope is that in the near future, there will be more female birds to produce healthy eggs and young.

SAVING
A SPECIES

Volunteers play a huge role in helping kakapo recovery efforts. During the breeding season, they make sure the birds are well fed by leaving food at different spots around the islands. Volunteers also camp near kakapo nests to keep an eye on mothers and their chicks. If anything goes wrong, they tell a team member. Each and every kakapo is precious and must be cared for.

A volunteer with a wild kakapo

Zoos have also contributed to kakapo **conservation**. The Auckland Zoo in New Zealand helps look after sick kakapos. The zoo staff also helps the Kakapo Recovery Programme by hand-raising chicks in captivity. In one year, the zoo helped raise dozens of chicks.

Each new chick is fed every four hours.

LOOK CLOSER

The volunteers who look after mothers and their chicks are called nest minders! They record how long mother birds are away from their nest, for example.

WORK TO DO

"We now have 210 birds in our **sanctuaries**, up from a low of 51 in 1995," says Andrew. However, the birds are still critically endangered. "My job is every conservation biologist's dream," he says. Using science, he can "make a real difference to the survival of an endangered species."

He knows that without constant attention, kakapos could become extinct within our lifetime. In fact, in 2019 a disease sickened 21 birds and killed 9. Andrew will continue fighting to save every last kakapo and give these strange and wonderful parrots a fighting chance. "We need to preserve animals like this, completely unique animals which are like nothing else on Earth," says Andrew. "It's our duty to save them."

LOOK CLOSER

"It's rewarding to work with this amazing species that most people never get to see," says Andrew. "People fall in love with kakapos when they know them."

FAST FACTS

KAKAPOS

Scientific Name
Strigops habroptilus

Physical Description
Mottled yellowish-green feathers with forward-facing eyes, gray beak, and short legs

Size
Up to 2 feet (61 centimeters) long and about 1 foot (30 cm) high

Weight
Up to 9 pounds (4 kg)

Main Diet
Plants including fruit, leaves, flowers, seeds, bark, and tubers

Habitat
Four small islands off the coast of New Zealand

Life Span
Unknown but an average of 60 years

DID YOU KNOW?

- Kakapos have large ears on their heads that are hidden under feathers.

- On their feet, kakapos have two toes pointing forward and two pointing backward.

- There are grooves inside a kakapo's beak, which help the bird chew fruit and get out the juice.

- A kakapo's strong musty scent comes from a special body part, called a gland, near their tail.

- Kakapos sometimes bite when they're afraid or grumpy. "Their bite is very painful, and they can draw a lot of blood," says Andrew.

GLOSSARY

aloof (uh-LOOF) not friendly; keeping at a distance

breed (BREED) to come together to have young

camouflage (KAM-uh-flahzh) a natural coloring or marking that allows an animal to hide by blending in with its surroundings

captivity (kap-TIV-ih-tee) places where animals live and are cared for by people, not in the animals' natural homes

conservation (kahn-sur-VAY-shuhn) the protection of wildlife and natural resources

conservation biologist (kahn-sur-VAY-shuhn bye-AH-luh-jist) a scientist who studies how best to protect wildlife and natural resources

depressions (dih-PRESH-uhnz) sunken places; areas lower than surrounding surfaces

endangered (en-DAYN-jurd) threatened with extinction, or dying out

evolved (ih-VOLVD) gradually changed over time due to a scientific process

extinction (ik-STINGKT-shuhn) when a type of animal dies out

flightless (FLITE-les) unable to fly

frequency (FREE-kwuhn-see) the rate at which vibration occurs to make a sound wave

genetic (juh-NET-ik) having to do with the way that an animal's characteristics are passed from one generation to another through genes

habitat (HAB-ih-tat) the natural home of an animal or plant

inbreeding (IN-breed-ing) the mating of closely related individuals

mate (MATE) a male or female partner; to come together to have young

minimize (MIN-uh-mize) to reduce something as much as possible

monitor (MAH-nihtur) to keep track of or watch carefully

mottled (MAHT-uld) spotted or blotched in coloring

musty (MUHS-tee) smelling of wetness or decay

nocturnal (nahk-TUR-nuhl) active mainly at night

parachute (PAH-ruh-shoot) a soft cloth attached to ropes that is used to slow down one's fall

population (pop-yuh-LAY-shuhn) the number of animals or people in a place

predators (PRED-uh-turz) animals that hunt and kill other animals for food

sanctuaries (SANGK-choo-er-eez) areas in nature where animals are protected from hunters and can live safely

strides (STRIDEZ) long steps animals take

transmitters (trans-MIT-erz) devices that send out radio waves to help scientists track an animal

tubers (TOO-buhrz) the thick underground stems of certain plants

volunteers (vah-luhn-TEERZ) people who do a job for no pay

READ MORE

Artell, Mike. *Pee-Yew: The Stinkiest, Smelliest Animals, Insects, and Plants on Earth!* Tucson: Good Year Books, 2007.

Hammond, Paula. *The Atlas of Endangered Animals.* Tarrytown, NY: Marshall Cavendish, 2010.

Zappa, Marcia. *Kakapos.* Mankato, MN: ABDO, 2008.

LEARN MORE ONLINE

Auckland Zoo: Wild Work for Kakapo
https://www.aucklandzoo.co.nz/news/wild-work-for-kakapo

New Zealand Birds Online: Kakapo
http://nzbirdsonline.org.nz/species/kakapo

New Zealand Department of Conservation: Kakapo Recovery
https://www.doc.govt.nz/our-work/kakapo-recovery

YouTube: Kakapo Conservation Field Work on Whenua Hou
https://www.youtube.com/watch?v=lb25oHMtUiU

INDEX

ABOUT THE AUTHOR

Joyce Markovics has authored more than 150 books for young readers. She's wild about rare and unusual animals and is passionate about preservation. Joyce lives in an old house along the Hudson River in Ossining, New York. She would like to thank Dr. Andrew Digby for his generous contribution to this book and for devoting his life to kakapo conservation.